HUNS

BARBARIANS!

Huns

KATHRYN HINDS

MARSHALL CAVENDISH · BENCHMARK · NEW YORK

In memory of Ter

The author and publisher specially wish to thank Charles W. King,
Associate Professor of History at the University of Nebraska, Omaha,
for his invaluable help in reviewing the manuscript of this book.

Marshall Cavendish Benchmark 99 White Plains Road Tarrytown, New York 10591
www.marshallcavendish.us
Text copyright © 2010 by Marshall Cavendish Corporation Map copyright © 2010 by Mike Reagan

LIBRARY OF CONGRESS CATALOGING-IN-PUBLICATION DATA
Hinds, Kathryn, 1962-
Huns / by Kathryn Hinds.
p. cm. — (Barbarians!)
Summary: "A history of the Huns, equestrian nomads of Central Asia
who pillaged Europe and Asia from the third through fifth centuries"—Provided by publisher.
Includes bibliographical references and index.
ISBN 978-0-7614-4066-6
1. Huns—History—Juvenile literature. 2. Attila, d. 453—Juvenile literature. 3. Nomads—Europe—History—Juvenile literature. 4. Nomads—Asia, Central—History—Juvenile literature. 5. Europe—History—To 476—Juvenile literature. 6. Asia, Central—History—Juvenile literature.
I. Title. D141.H56 2010   936'.03—dc22   2008054828

EDITOR: Joyce Stanton PUBLISHER: Michelle Bisson ART DIRECTOR: Anahid Hamparian SERIES DESIGNER: Michael Nelson

Printed in Malaysia
135642

front cover: Attila, king of the Huns, in a painting by nineteenth-century French artist Eugène Delacroix
half-title page: A fifth-century coin from what is now Afghanistan portrays one of the rulers of the White Huns.
title page: Attila, surrounded by his men, from a painting by Raphael
page 6: A first-century BCE silver plaque from Mongolia, possibly the ancient homeland of the Huns
back cover: A Mongolian silver harness decoration from the first century BCE showing a yak

CONTENTS

WHO WERE THE BARBARIANS?

THE HISTORY OF THE ANCIENT WORLD IS DOMINATED BY the city-based societies of Greece, Rome, China, India, and others. Yet not far beyond the borders of these famed civilizations lived other peoples: the barbarians. They were first given this name by the ancient Greeks, imitating the sounds of languages that the Greeks found incomprehensible. Soon, though, barbarians came to be thought of not just as peoples unfamiliar with the languages and customs of Greece and Rome, but as wild, uncivilized, uncultured peoples. This stereotype has largely endured to the present day, and the barbarian label has been applied to a variety of peoples from many parts of Europe and Asia.

The barbarians, of course, did not think of themselves this way. They had rich cultures of their own, as even some ancient writers realized. Great Greek and Roman historians such as Herodotus and Tacitus investigated and described their customs, sometimes even holding them up as examples for the people of their own sophisticated societies. Moreover, the relationships between the barbarians and civilization were varied and complex. Barbarians are most famous for raiding and invading, and these were certainly among their activities. But often the barbarians were peaceable neighbors and close allies, trading with the more settled peoples and even serving them as soldiers and contributing to their societies in other ways.

Our information about the barbarians comes from a variety of sources: archaeology, language studies, ancient and medieval historians, and later literature. Unfortunately, though, we generally have few records in the barbarians' own words, since most of these peoples left little written material. Instead we frequently learn about them from the writings of civilizations who thought of them as strange and usually inferior, and often as enemies. But modern scholars, like detectives, have been sifting through the evidence to learn more and more about these peoples and the compelling roles they played in the history of Europe, Asia, and even Africa. Now it's our turn to look beyond the borders of the familiar civilizations of the past and meet the barbarians.

A variety of systems of dating have been used by different cultures throughout history. Many historians now prefer to use BCE (Before Common Era) and CE (Common Era) instead of BC (Before Christ) and AD (Anno Domini), out of respect for the diversity of the world's peoples.

INTRODUCING the HUNS

TOWARD THE END OF THE FOURTH CENTURY, A RETIRED ROMAN soldier named Ammianus Marcellinus set out to write a history of the Roman Empire from the end of the first century to his own time. He composed the final volume in 395. Twenty years earlier, he recalled, "a race of men, hitherto unknown, had suddenly descended like a whirlwind from the lofty mountains, as if they had risen from some secret recess of the earth, and were ravaging and destroying everything which came in their way." These previously unknown people were the Huns.

MYSTERIES AND BEGINNINGS

The Huns have long been some of history's most famous barbarians. Yet there are some very basic things about them that we don't know. For example, what was their language? There is no Hunnish literature of any kind—as the sixth-century historian Procopius wrote, the Huns were "absolutely unacquainted with writing and unskilled in it to the present day. They have neither writing masters nor do the children

Opposite page: Attila, the Huns' most famous king, portrayed as the stereotype of the rampaging barbarian

among them toil over the letters at all as they grow up." Only a few Hunnish words are known, for example *strava*, meaning "funeral." The Hun names recorded by authors of the time show influences from several language families, including Germanic and Iranian. A majority of the names, however, seem likely to be Turkic. This has led many modern scholars to conclude that the Huns spoke a language related to modern Turkish, but no one can be absolutely certain of this.

Another thing we're not sure about is exactly where the Huns originated. When Greek and Roman writers first heard of them, they were living north of the Caucasus Mountains, between the Sea of Azov and the Volga River. But this area had long been home to a people called the Alans, so the Huns must have come there from somewhere else. Historians generally agree that the "somewhere else" was Central Asia—modern Kazakhstan, Turkmenistan, Uzbekistan, Tajikistan, Kyrgyzstan, and China's Xinjiang Province.*

Through Central Asia ran part of the Eurasian steppe, the band of dry, flat grasslands that stretched all the way from Hungary to Mongolia. During ancient and medieval times, the steppes were home to a number of different peoples, many of them nomads. The steppes were generally too dry to support farming, but the grasses could feed a variety of livestock. A group of nomads typically ranged over a wide territory, herding their animals from one pasture to another according to the availability of grass during different seasons. Most nomads had close ties with farm villages around the steppes' edges, trading livestock and livestock products for grain and other produce. But in unsettled times, nomads frequently resorted to raiding rather than trading. For some groups, such as the Huns, raiding became a regular and important part of the nomadic way of life.

*This large region is sometimes known as Turkestan—the country or homeland of the Turks. Turkish peoples did not start settling in the country now known as Turkey until the eleventh century.

THE NORTHERN HORSE BARBARIANS

Some scholars have traced the Huns back from Central Asia to an even more distant time and place. Ancient Chinese writings described a people known as the Xiongnu (or Hsiung-nu), which is sometimes translated as "northern horse barbarians." They lived north of China, in what is now Mongolia. Some language experts believe that *Xiongnu* and *Hun* are probably related terms. Moreover, in records from the fourth century they were used to describe the same people. Archaeologists have also made discoveries that may link the Xiongnu and the Huns. For example, both groups had a particular type of metal cauldron, which they typically buried (for unknown reasons) beside rivers.

Above: The Mongolian steppe, painted by a twentieth-century artist but virtually unchanged since the time of the Xiongnu
Below: This bronze cauldron, found in what is now Hungary, was used by the Huns in the fifth century CE.

Like the later Huns and other steppe nomads, the Xiongnu herded their livestock from horseback. Their riding skills were impressive, and they were also expert archers. While riding at top speed, they could shoot arrow after arrow with astonishingly accurate aim. These abilities were the result of training that began in toddlerhood, when boys climbed onto the backs of sheep for their first riding lessons and learned to shoot rodents and birds with miniature bows and arrows. As they got older, they graduated to horses and to hunting such fast-moving animals as foxes and hares. They were considered adults only when they had the strength to use a man's bow.

The Xiongnu's skills in horsemanship and archery made them great hunters and fearsome warriors. During the third century BCE they raided the kingdoms of northern China so often that the Chinese rulers built walls along their borders in the hope of stopping, or at least slowing, the attacks. When these Chinese kingdoms united under a single emperor in 221 BCE, their defenses were joined together to form the beginning of the Great Wall. Even this was not a completely effective barrier against the Xiongnu. But it did discourage small raiding parties, and it provided a fortified base for Chinese defense forces in times of trouble.

Nomads in Xinjiang Province continued the ancient lifestyle of the steppes well into the twentieth century.

THE LAMENT OF LIU CHI-HSÜN

FROM BEHIND THE SECURITY OF THE GREAT WALL, CHINESE RULERS FREQUENTLY sent princesses and highborn ladies to marry Xiongnu chieftains as part of efforts to keep the peace. Around 100 BCE a lady named Liu Chi-hsün went to live with the Wusun, a steppe tribe allied to the Xiongnu, and wrote this lament:

My family married me off

to the King of the Wusun,

and I live in an alien land

a million miles from nowhere.

My house is a tent.

My walls are of felt.

Raw flesh is all I eat,

with horse milk to drink.

I always think of home

and my heart stings.

O to be a yellow snow-goose

floating home again!

By the time the Great Wall was built, the Xiongnu were a confederation of tribes ruled by a king called the *shanyu*. Perhaps the strongest, most dynamic *shanyu* was Maodun, who came to power in 209 BCE. He solidified the Xiongnu confederation, which had been wavering, and then led them in a crushing victory over the Chinese emperor. After taking over land south of the Great Wall, the Xiongnu began extending their influence into the steppes to the west. By the 160s BCE they were the overlords of eastern Central Asia. A Chinese historian observed, "Whenever a Xiongnu envoy appeared in the region carrying credentials from the Shanyu, he was escorted from state to state and provided with food, and no one dared to detain him or cause him any difficulty."

Ch'in Shih Huang Ti united seven Chinese kingdoms to become China's first emperor in 221 BCE. He then turned his attention to defending his new empire from the Xiongnu.

The Xiongnu collected so much grain and other tribute from their subjects that they built towns where these things could be stored. Towns were also centers of trade and administration. Some Xiongnu settled down in villages as farmers and craftspeople. Upper-class Xiongnu were buried in tombs filled with luxuries from China and beyond. During life, however, many of the nomads failed to appreciate these finer things, at least according to a Chinese ambassador to the Xiongnu: "They have no desire for our things. We have sent them silk costumes; they have worn them to shreds hunting in thickets and then declared that silk was not as good as their hides.

We have sent them delicacies to eat; they have found them infinitely inferior to their milk and koumiss."*

During the 50s BCE the Xiongnu confederation fell apart, with the tribes split between a number of *shanyu*. Within a few years there were only two *shanyu* left, one ruling north and west of Mongolia's Gobi Desert and the other in the south. Those in the south soon bowed to the authority of the Chinese emperor, and their territory became part of China. The remaining Xiongnu continued to war against China, with occasional periods of peace. In 48 CE these Xiongnu, too, split into two groups. The new Southern Xiongnu settled in northern China but lived under the rule of their own *shanyu* till the early third century. In the early fourth century they raided the Chinese capital and helped bring about the downfall of the ruling dynasty.

Meanwhile, the Northern Xiongnu played a dominant role in eastern Central Asia for some time, their armies active in many of the major cities. China, however, also wanted control of this region. Toward the end of the first century CE, the Chinese drove the Northern Xiongnu from their power base in Mongolia. While many of the Xiongnu surrendered to China, the *shanyu* and several thousand followers went west to settle in what is now southeastern Kazakhstan. They continued to make forays into western China well into the second century.

After 153 CE, Chinese records make no further mention of the Xiongnu's presence in eastern Central Asia. Could this be because they had moved farther west, slowly migrating toward the region where the Huns first became known to the Romans in the 300s? We will probably never know for certain. Nevertheless, some historians think it possible that the "hitherto unknown" Huns described by Ammianus Marcellinus were descendants of the Xiongnu, mixed with various other peoples encountered during the course of their journeys.

*Koumiss is a drink made from fermented mare's milk. It was an important part of the diet for many different groups of steppe nomads.

"HEAVEN WAS PITILESS"

THE SOUTHERN XIONGNU LIVED PEACEABLY WITHIN CHINA FOR MANY YEARS, until the Chinese government became unstable in the late second century. Then the Xiongnu took the opportunity to expand their territory and raid their neighbors. During the raiding, the poet Ts'ai Yen was captured and taken away to the north. She expressed her grief in a number of poems, including the following selection (in which the translator has used *Tatars* as a generic name for the horse-riding archers who terrorized Ts'ai Yen and her people).

Heaven was pitiless.
It sent down confusion and separation.
Earth was pitiless.
It brought me to birth in such a time.
War was everywhere. Every road was dangerous.
Soldiers and civilians everywhere
Fleeing death and suffering.
Smoke and dust obscured the land
Overrun by the ruthless Tartar bands.
Our people lost their will power and integrity.
I can never learn the ways of the barbarians. . . .
A Tartar chief forced me to become his wife,
And took me far away to Heaven's edge.
Ten thousand clouds and mountains
Bar my road home.
And whirlwinds of dust and sand
Blow for a thousand miles.
Men here are as savage as giant vipers,
And strut about in armour, snapping their bows.
As I sing the second stanza I almost break the lutestrings,
Will broken, heart broken, I sing to myself.

HUNS IN PERSIAN LANDS?

From the 220s to the mid-600s, a powerful Persian state called the Sasanian Empire dominated the lands from Iraq to the edge of India. On the empire's northeastern border lay a region called Sogdiana, roughly modern Tajikistan and eastern Uzbekistan. This was a meeting place of Persian and Central Asian cultures, where many peoples mingled. By the fourth century, these peoples probaby included Huns.

Around 350 a tribe or tribal coalition known as the Chionites advanced from Sogdiana into the Sasanian Empire. They seem to have taken over the city of Balkh in northern Afghanistan and to have used that as a power base to bring the surrounding area under their control. By 356 the Sasanian emperor Shapur II was fully occupied fighting the Chionites. Two years later, however, he made a treaty with them and began enlisting Chionite units in his army. In 359 Chionites fought with the Sasanians against the Romans in what is now eastern Turkey. The next year a city in western Syria was besieged by perhaps this same group of Chionites—but the Syrian writer who recorded the event referred to the attackers as Huns.

The name *Chionite* may be related to *Hun* (often spelled *Chuni* in ancient sources—in both words, the *ch* was pronounced like a harsh *h* in the back of the throat). Scholars have disagreed, however, over whether or not the Chionites were Huns, partly because their lan-

This nearly lifesize portrait of Shapur II, made from a single piece of silver by a fourth-century Persian artist, conveys the pride and majesty of the Sasanian empire and its ruler.

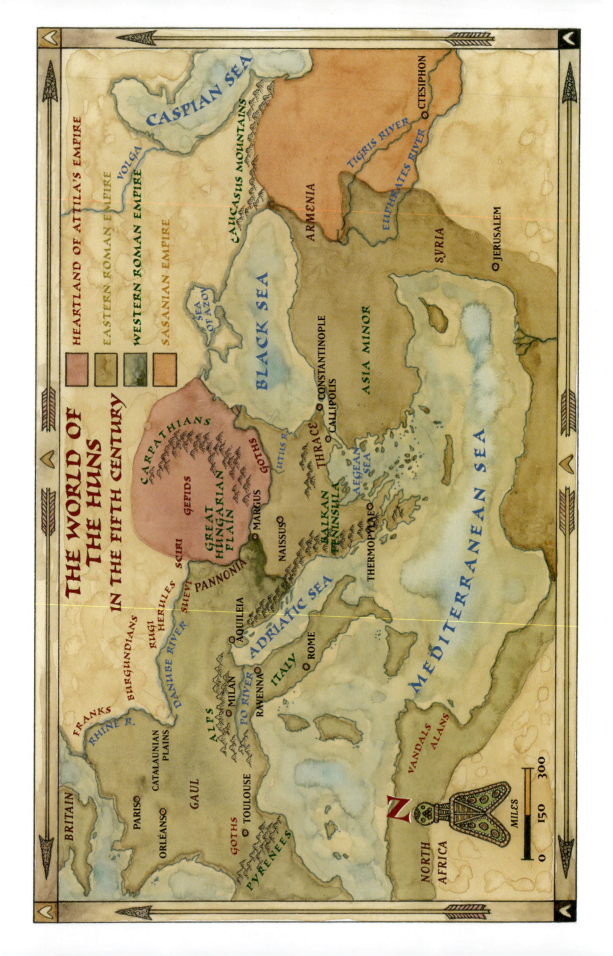

guage seems to have been Iranian. Moreover, Ammianus Marcellinus wrote about both Chionites and Huns, and never connected them with each other. Yet according to Chinese historical traditions, the Xiongnu settled in and eventually dominated Sogdiana, and Persian and Indian sources provide links between the Chionites and peoples referred to (for unknown reasons) as Red Huns and White Huns. So some modern authors think it possible that the Chionites at least had Huns among them, even if on the whole they were not the same people as the Huns who would soon make their first impact on Europe.

PEOPLES on the MOVE

N 363 THE ROMAN EMPEROR MADE PEACE WITH SHAPUR II, and the treaty stated that their two empires should join together to protect the passes through the Caucasus Mountains against invasions by, in Roman words, "those barbarians who are unknown both to us and to the Persians." Modern scholars have different opinions about just who "those barbarians" were. Some think they were "Black Huns" or Kidarites, who, they say, were not related to the Huns that would soon become known to the Romans.*

The confusion arises because surviving writings from this period of history give us many names of peoples but not enough information to be sure of who was who and what they were doing and where they were doing it. That is, until 376—the year that, in the words of Ammianus Marcellinus, "a terrible rumour arose that . . . a barbarian host composed of different distant nations, which had suddenly been driven

*Opinions on the Kidarites differ, too: some authors consider them to have been an offshoot of the Chionites, and others refer to them as the first of several groups of "Iranian Huns" to migrate south from Central Asia.

Opposite page: A marble sculpture of a barbarian horseman from the region around the Black Sea and lower Danube River

21

by force from their own country, was now . . . wandering about in different directions on the banks of the river Danube."

The rumor proved to be true. The wandering barbarians were Goths, members of a group of eastern Germanic tribes. But (according to Ammianus), "the seed-bed and origin of all this destruction and of the various calamities inflicted by the wrath of Mars [the Roman war god], which raged everywhere with extraordinary fury, I find to be this: the people of the Huns."

NEW PASTURES

Gothic tribes had long been settled just west of the Sea of Azov, north of the Black Sea in what is now southern Ukraine. According to a Gothic legend, the Huns on the other side of the Sea of Azov did not know about the Goths or their lands—until one of the Huns' cows was bitten by a fly. Provoked by the bite, the cow ran away across the marshes and the narrow strait connecting the Sea of Azov and the Black Sea. A Hun herder followed her, and she led him into the rich Gothic pastures. The herder naturally went back and told his fellow Huns, and they set out to conquer the Goths. In another version of this legend, it was a deer, followed by a party of Hun hunters, who led the way into the territory of the Goths. However the Huns found out about the pastures north of the Black Sea, their neighbors' "greener grass" beckoned.

Around 370, Hun warriors rode north and crossed into lands occupied by the Alans. Then, "having traversed the territory of the Alani, and having slain many of them and acquired much plunder, [the Huns] made a treaty of friendship and alliance with those who remained. And when they had united them to themselves, with increased boldness they made sudden incursion into the fertile districts of Ermenrichus"— Ermenaric, ruler of one of the Gothic tribes. Ammianus went on to tell how Ermenaric and his successors tried to resist the onslaught of the

Huns and their Alan allies. Meanwhile, other groups of Goths became increasingly nervous about this new threat from the east.

A large number of Goths—entire families, perhaps as many as 200,000 people in all—decided to leave their tribal lands and seek safety within the Roman Empire. In 376 they reached what is now Romania and asked for permission to cross the Danube River into Roman territory. The emperor granted their request, but the region could not handle such a huge influx of refugees. There was not enough food for them, and Roman officials tried to exploit and cheat them. Many of the Goths turned to raiding to support themselves. Soon the Roman army was sent in to deal with them.

By autumn 377, the Romans had the Goths trapped in the mountains of the eastern Balkan Peninsula. Somehow, though, the Goths managed to send envoys to the Huns and Alans. Lured by the promise of immense plunder, they agreed to ride to the Goths' aid. When the Roman commander learned the Huns and Alans were on their way, he ordered his men to retreat, leaving the Balkan passes open. Then, in the words of Ammianus, "the barbarians, like beasts who had broken

An 1873 illustration of the Huns— portrayed here as a people similar to the Mongols of later history—in battle with the Alans. The Huns' weapons include lassos, which, as Ammianus Marcellinus wrote, they used to entangle their enemies "so that they lose the ability to ride or walk."

loose from their cages, poured unrestrainedly over the vast extent of the country." They looted towns and villas, "spreading ravage, slaughter, bloodshed, and conflagration [fire], and throwing everything into the foulest disorder by all sorts of acts of violence."

The following year, 378, the Goths won a great victory against the Romans, with two-thirds of the Roman army and the emperor himself killed in the battle.* A contingent of Huns and Alans was still fighting on the Gothic side, and continued raiding the northern Balkan Peninsula for the next year or so. Roman authors wrote of the "roving fierceness of the Huns" and commented that they were "more violent in every destruction" than other barbarians.

The Huns who went west in the 370s do not seem to have been united under a single leader. Instead, individual Hun war bands each pursued their own interests. (Early on, some groups of Huns even fought as mercenaries on the side of the Goths against their fellow

Some scholars think that the Huns who moved into the Great Hungarian Plain largely abandoned the nomadic lifestyle. This is an artist's impression of a fortified Hun settlement in central Europe.

*For more of the Goths' story, see *Goths*, another volume in this series.

Huns.) The number of Huns in central Europe was still fairly small, as the majority of the population seems to have remained in their lands north of the Caucasus Mountains. By the 380s, however, it is likely that some Huns, together with their allies and subjects, were using what is now eastern Hungary as a base of operations. Over the following decades, more and more Huns would migrate onto the Great Hungarian Plain, where they would settle down permanently and become the region's dominant power.

ALLIES AND ENEMIES

When the Huns entered Roman history, the empire was not the strong, unified state it had once been. In fact, it was in the process of splitting into two parts, each with its own emperor. The dividing line was in the western Balkan Peninsula. The Western Empire was no longer ruled from Rome, but from Ravenna, in northern Italy. The capital of the Eastern Empire was Constantinople (modern Istanbul, Turkey). The two halves of the empire had been growing apart in other ways—for example, Latin was the common language of the West, while most people in the East used Greek. The East was more stable, while the West tended to be troubled by rebellions, usurpers, and repeated barbarian invasions.

In 384 a West Roman commander enlisted a troop of Hun and Alan cavalry as allies. Their task was to drive off a Germanic tribe that was attacking the Roman province that is now Switzerland. The horsemen crushed the invading Germans easily. But instead of turning around and going home, they kept on riding west, making for the rich provinces of Gaul (modern France and Belgium). The Roman commander was able to stop them only by paying them a large sum of gold—the first recorded instance of Romans buying peace from the Huns.

In 388 the emperor of the East, Theodosius I, went to war against a general who had usurped the throne of the Western Empire. To strengthen his army, Theodosius "accepted the barbarian peoples who vowed to lend him their help as fellow combatants." The alliance also served to keep these peoples— including the Huns—from threatening his borders, at least for the time being. The barbarian troops served even better than expected, as recorded by a writer named Pacatus:

O memorable thing: There marched under Roman leaders and banners . . . those who before had been our enemies, . . . and as soldiers filled the cities of Pannonia [western Hungary] which they had emptied with fiendish devastation. Goths and Huns and Alans answered the roll call, changed guards, and rarely feared to be reprimanded. There was no tumult, no confusion, no looting in the usual barbarian way.

Above: Theodosius I presides over a church council in Constantinople.

Right: A mosaic in Ravenna shows a group of Theodosius I's soldiers.

Theodosius won his war. In the aftermath, however, a number of the barbarian allies deserted and turned to raiding once more. Things got so bad in the Balkan Peninsula that in 391 Theodosius was back on the battlefield, this time to put down the brigands, among whom were many Huns as well as Goths, Alans, and others. The fighting was dreadful, but at the end Theodosius seems to have made peace with the surviving barbarians. As a result, a group of Huns were settled on lands in Thrace (roughly modern Bulgaria) in return for promising to fight for the empire when needed. Another group of Huns, however, was about to seriously threaten the Eastern Empire's peace.

FORAYS INTO ASIA

In July 395 a large number of Huns crossed the Caucasus Mountains and rode south into some of the East's richest provinces. They seem to have been driven to this course of action by a famine in their land. They also took advantage of the fact that a civil war in Italy had tied up much of the Roman army, leaving the passes through the Caucasus poorly defended. The Huns raided Armenia and eastern Asia Minor, then plundered the countryside and some of the cities of Syria. Afterward they crossed the Euphrates River and, according to a Syrian historian, "the bridge was cut off and the troops of the Romans gathered from various sides against them and annihilated them, and no one of the Huns escaped."

In a letter the following year, Saint Jerome, living as a hermit in Bethlehem, described that terrifying summer:

> Lo, suddenly messengers ran to and fro and the whole East trembled, for swarms of Huns had broken forth from the far distant Maeotis [the Sea of Azov]. . . . They filled the whole earth with slaughter and panic alike as they flitted hither and thither on their swift horses. . . . They were at hand everywhere before they were expected: by their speed they outstripped rumour, and they took pity neither upon religion nor rank nor age nor wailing childhood.

Originally from Italy, Saint Jerome settled in Bethlehem in 384, where he lived for the rest of his life.

The Eastern Romans were not the only people to suffer Hun attacks in 395. A second group of Huns also crossed the Caucasus that year. Led by chiefs named Basich and Kursich, they headed further southeast, into the Sasanian Empire. Although the adventure was not completely successful, it was well remembered among the Huns. More than fifty years later, East Roman ambassadors to the court of Attila the Hun were told:

> Basich and Kursich, . . . rulers of a vast horde, advanced into the land of the Medes [Persians]. . . . A Persian host came on them as they were plundering and overrunning the land and, being on higher ground than they, filled the air with [arrows], so that, encompassed by danger, the Huns had to retreat and retire across the mountains with little loot, for the greatest part was seized by the Medes.

These events also lived on in the memories of the people of the region, and a Syrian chronicle from a century or two later adds some additional details of the Huns' activities:

> They descended to the banks of the Euphrates and Tigris in the territory of the Persians and came as far as the royal city of the Persians.* They did no damage there but devastated many districts on the Euphrates and Tigris, killed many people and led many into captivity. But when they learned that the Persians advanced against them, they turned to flight. The Persians chased them and killed a band. They took away all their plunder and liberated eighteen thousand prisoners.

ULDIN

Basich and Kursich are among the earliest Hun leaders we know by name. Another was Uldin, who ruled a group of Huns in what is now eastern Romania. In 400 he and his warriors helped out the East Romans by fighting a group of rebellious Goths and killing their leader.

*Ctesiphon, the capital of the Sasanian Empire. It was located approximately where Baghdad is today.

During the winter of 404–405, however, Uldin led his men across the frozen Danube into the empire in a lightning raid on Thrace. Then in early 406 Uldin and his followers went to the aid of the Western Empire, which desperately needed their assistance to drive invading Goths out of Italy. The Hun cavalry swiftly outflanked the Gothic forces, allowing Roman troops to move in for the kill. The Huns took many prisoners, whom they sold as slaves. But the profits seem to have lasted them only so long, because in 408 Uldin's Huns were plundering Thrace again.

The raids devastated the region and struck fear into people as far away as Jerusalem, where Saint Jerome wrote that the attacks of these "savage tribes whose face and language is terrifying" must have been permitted by God in order to punish the unfaithful. Most of the East Roman army had been sent away from the Balkans to strengthen the empire's border with Persia, so the commander in Thrace did not have enough troops to counter the Huns. He tried, therefore, to negotiate a peace with Uldin. The Hun leader answered by pointing toward the rising sun and proclaiming that he would subdue every land it shone on, unless the Romans paid him a large amount of gold. Unfortunately for Uldin, a great number of his men decided to accept the peace settlement and joined the Roman side. Those who remained were either killed in battle or taken prisoner and sold as slaves in Constantinople.

Uldin escaped back to his lands north of the Danube, where his later activities can only be guessed at. Some historians believe he expanded his control west into Hungary—in any case, it seems that by the 410s the Great Hungarian Plain was the center of the Huns' power and population. Other scholars think Uldin focused on bringing the Gepids, a nearby Germanic tribe, under Hun rule. Still other writers point out that because he had lost so many men in Thrace, he may have lost much of his authority. Huns, like other steppe nomads, did not follow their leaders with unquestioning obedience. Chiefs had to constantly earn their followers' respect and loyalty, through success and generosity.

THE HUNS "WERE TOTALLY INCAPABLE AND IGNORANT OF CONDUCTING A BATTLE on foot, but by wheeling, charging, retreating in good time and shooting from their horses, they wrought immense slaughter." The Greek author who wrote this pinpointed the secret of the Huns' success as warriors and raiders: their superior skill in both horsemanship and archery. The two abilities were developed through long practice.

HORSE AND BOW

Hun children got their first riding lessons very young, with results that were observed by the fifth-century poet Sidonius Apollinaris: "Scarcely has the infant learned to stand, without its mother's help, when a horse takes him on his back. You would think that the limbs of the man and horse were born together, so firmly does the rider always stick to the horse. Other people are carried on horseback; these people live there."

Above: Ammianus wrote that the Huns were "almost glued to their horses," and in this dramatic painting the rider has such complete control of his mount, he doesn't even need reins.

The horses themselves were bred for particular qualities that served the Huns well, even though Romans thought the animals were unattractive. The late-fourth-century military theorist Vegetius described them this way:

The Hunnish horses have large heads, curved like hooks, protruding eyes, narrow nostrils, broad jaws, strong and rigid necks. Their manes hang down to their knees, their ribs are big, their backbones curved, and their tails shaggy. . . . The stature is rather long than tall. The trunk is vaulted, and the bones are strong, and the leanness of the horses is striking. But one forgets the ugly appearance of these horses as this is set off by their fine qualities: their sober nature, cleverness and their ability to endure any injuries very well.

The Huns' bows were equally special. Like other Central Asian nomads, the Huns used what is called a composite recurve bow. The "composite" part means that the bow was made of a combination of materials—wood, sinew, and horn or bone—layered in sections or thin strips and glued together. It could take nearly a year to produce such a bow, which had to be made in stages to provide time for the wood and sinew to cure and the glue to dry. The time and effort were worthwhile, though, because the composite construction gave the bow the strength and flexibility necessary for the recurve shape. This means that an unstrung bow curved in the opposite direction from when it was strung. Bending the bow into the proper position to string it created a high amount of tension in both bow and string. That tension was stored-up energy, which gave the bow immense power.

Hun bows were even more powerful than those of earlier steppe warriors because they were much longer. Normally a long bow is difficult or impossible to shoot from horseback. But the Huns refined the design of their bow to solve this problem. They added extra length to the top section of the weapon, keeping the bottom section short enough to avoid bumping into the horse's neck or tangling in the reins. A Hun bow therefore had the range and power to shoot arrows that could pierce armor from as far away as a hundred yards—the length of an entire football field. Against unarmored opponents, Hun archers could be effective across the same distance as two football fields.

The RISE of ATTILA

ALTHOUGH ULDIN MADE GREAT PROGRESS ON STRENGTHENING the Huns across the Roman frontier, he had not united all the Huns. For example, in 409 a number of Huns joined a Gothic army that moved into the western Balkan Peninsula. The Roman commander sent to drive them out had his own band of three hundred Huns, who killed more than a thousand of the invaders while losing only seventeen of their own men. Later in the year another group of Goths threatened to march on the city of Rome, and the emperor summoned a large number of Hun auxiliaries into Italy to deter the Gothic advance.

Around 411 the Western Empire appears to have made a treaty with some of the Huns. As part of the terms the two sides exchanged hostages, who would function as goodwill ambassadors and insurance that each party would stick to the agreement. One of the Romans who went to live among the Huns was a teenager named Flavius Aetius. He stayed with them for three years, learning their customs and language. This experience would come in handy later, as he rose in importance in the Roman government and army.

Opposite page: The sixteenth-century artist who painted this picture titled it *Attila, Flagellum Dei*— "Attila, the Scourge of God." The nickname, given to the Hun leader during the eighth or ninth century, has lasted into modern times.

In 425 Aetius was in the service of a usurping emperor of the West named John, who was opposed by the Eastern emperor. So "John sent Aetius with a great sum of gold to the Huns, a people known to him since the time when he was their hostage and attached to him by a close friendship." The ancient author tells us that he brought 60,000 Huns to fight for John. The number was probably more like 6,000—but even so, this was a very large number of Hun warriors united for the same purpose. We can guess, therefore, that different groups of Huns had been joining together into a new confederation under strong and successful leadership.

A ROYAL FAMILY

Aetius, as imagined by an artist in the 1500s

By the mid to late 420s, three brothers were in power in the lands north of the lower Danube. Named Octar (or Uptar), Rua (or Ruga), and Mundiuch, each ruled his own territory. Their subjects included not just Huns but also various Germanic peoples. The German warriors who fought for the Huns were generally foot soldiers armed with swords and spears. A number of Alans were still under Hun rule as well, although most had broken away and migrated westward in the early 400s. Alan warriors were heavy cavalry whose main weapons were long lances and swords. Both they and their horses wore armor into combat, in contrast to the Huns, who fought with little armor and relied on speed and maneuverability.

Octar's realm was apparently the westernmost of the three Hun kingdoms. He seems to have made frequent raids on the Germanic peoples living to the northwest, particularly the Burgundians. Around 430 he launched his final foray against them. According to a historian of the time, on the eve of battle Octar "burst asunder in the night" as a result of too much food and drink, and "the Burgundians attacked that people [the Huns] then without a leader; and although few in numbers and their opponents many, they obtained a victory . . . and destroyed no less than 10,000 of the enemy." The number is almost certainly exaggerated, but the defeat was nevertheless a blow to the Huns' pride—one that would be avenged in the future.

Rua may have taken over Octar's territory. At any rate, he is the brother we know most about, thanks largely to his connections with Rome. In 432 Rua welcomed Aetius back among the Huns. After falling out of favor with the empress Galla Placidia, who ruled the West as regent for her son, Aetius had survived a murder attempt by a rival general. Now he wanted Rua's help. The Hun king granted his request, probably in return for substantial payments—which may have included not only money but also land in Pannonia, south of the Danube. The next year Aetius returned to Italy, apparently backed by a troop of Huns. We don't know what exactly happened, but we do know that Aetius regained his position as head of the West Roman army.

A portrayal of Galla Placidia on a coin issued while she was regent for her son

Aside from his dealings with Aetius, most of Rua's attention was directed to the Eastern Empire. The details are sketchy, but Rua seems to have conducted a war or at least a series of raids in the Balkans. In any case, the result was a treaty that required the East Romans to pay him an annual tribute of 350 pounds of gold in order to keep the peace. This tribute was paid directly to Rua, and then he shared the gold out to the chiefs under him. It was a great way for him to win, keep, and reward loyalty, and no doubt helped him increase his power immensely.

In spite of the gold, not all the Huns of his kingdom wanted to be ruled by Rua. Some of them fled across the Danube and offered their military services to Theodosius II, the emperor of the East. Rua sent an ambassador to Theodosius to demand that these and other Hun fugitives be sent back to him. If they were not, Rua would regard the peace treaty as broken. Negotiations must have collapsed, because Huns seem to have been back to raiding Thrace (or preparing to do so) when Rua died, sometime after the end of 435. Rua's power passed to two brothers, his nephews. They had already inherited the kingdom of their father, Mundiuch, who had died sometime earlier. Their names were Bleda and Attila.

THE BROTHERS

In 438, at Margus in what is now Serbia, East Roman diplomats met with the new Hun rulers. The historian Priscus noted that the Huns did not "think it proper to confer dismounted, so that the Romans, mindful of their own dignity, chose to meet [them] in the same fashion, lest one side speak from horseback, the other on foot."

Bleda and Attila were able to negotiate a new treaty that was even better for the Huns than Rua's had been. The tribute was doubled to seven hundred pounds of gold a year. In addition, the Romans promised to send back all Hun fugitives and not to allow any more into the empire; to return all Roman prisoners of war who had escaped from the Huns or else pay a ransom for each of them; to give the Huns the same trading rights, terms, and guarantees of safety as Romans at the markets held along the Danube; and not to make any alliances with the Huns' enemies. For the next couple years, therefore, the Huns left the Eastern Empire alone, and Attila seems to have focused on extending his and Bleda's authority to the north and east.

Meanwhile, with regard to the Western Empire, Attila and Bleda apparently honored Rua's agreement with Aetius, who still had Hun troops working for him. In 437, urged on for unknown reasons by Aetius, the Huns attacked the Burgundians and destroyed their kingdom along the Rhine River. One historian of the time said that 20,000 Burgundians were killed, including their king. Aetius also employed Hun cavalry against rebels in northern Gaul and Goths in southern Gaul. The end of this alliance came in 439, when the Goths defeated Aetius's lieutenant outside the city of Toulouse, and all the Huns under the lieutenant's command were killed. Aetius would get no more help from the Huns.

The Romans, East and West, had their hands full with other matters in any case. In October 439 a combined army of Vandals (a Germanic people) and Alans conquered the Western Empire's territories in North Africa—territories that supplied Italy with most of its grain. The two Roman empires began to put together a joint force, under Aetius's command, to deal with the situation. At the same time, the East suffered renewed attacks along its border with the Sasanian Empire. With so many military needs elsewhere, troops were pulled away from the Danube frontier and the Balkans—an opportunity that the Huns immediately seized.

During a trade fair in the winter of 440–441, Huns attacked a Roman fort on the north bank of the Danube. When the East Romans accused them of breaking the treaty, Attila and Bleda declared that the Romans had already broken it: they had not been paying the annual tribute and they still hadn't turned over all the Hun fugitives. Moreover, the Hun leaders said, "the bishop of Margus had crossed over to their land, and searching out their royal tombs, had stolen the valuables stored there."

Gem-encrusted gold tiaras like this one have been found in more than twenty graves of Hun women. Most of these high-status headdresses were discovered in the region north of the Black Sea, but this one came from Hungary.

The Huns demanded that the Romans make their payments, send back the fugitives, and hand over the grave-robbing bishop of Margus, or there would be war. The Romans did not give in.

In spring 441 the Huns crossed the Danube and captured or destroyed a series of frontier forts and towns, including a major military base that they completely demolished. As they approached Margus, the bishop panicked. He went secretly to Attila and Bleda to bargain for his life, offering to hand his city over to them; naturally they accepted. The bishop returned home, and on an agreed-upon night opened the city gates to the invading Huns. What happened to him afterward is unknown, but Margus was razed to the ground.

The Huns now had access to one of the empire's main military roads through the Balkans. They plundered a number of towns and cities along its route. Unlike previous barbarian attackers, they were not stopped by walls and other strong defenses. Thanks to their alliances with Roman forces, they knew how to use siege engines to break down city walls. This was what they did to the fortress-city of Naissus in 442. Naissus was a key military center because it guarded the place where the road forked, with one branch leading straight to Constantinople itself.

At this point, however, the Huns did not push through to the Eastern Empire's capital. Aetius and his army had been recalled to defend the Balkans (therefore leaving North Africa in the hands of the Vandals and Alans), but had not yet arrived. So after the Huns seized Naissus, the East Romans bought themselves more time by negotiating another treaty, which probably doubled the annual tribute payment. The Huns returned, for the time being, to their lands north of the Danube. There they had conflicts of their own to deal with. We don't know the details, but we do know the result: in 444 or 445, Attila had Bleda killed.

Attila was now the sole ruler of the Hun confederacy. And he received a sign that seemed to promise even more, as Priscus was told when he visited Attila's headquarters a few years later:

A certain herdsman saw one of his heifers limping. Unable to find a cause for such a wound, he anxiously followed the trail of blood and at length came to a sword the beast had unwittingly trampled while grazing. He dug it up and straight away took it to Attila. He [Attila] rejoiced at this gift and being of great courage he decided he had been appointed to be ruler of the whole world and that, thanks to the Sword of Mars,* he had been granted the power to win wars.

THE WAR OF 447

Around the time of Bleda's death, the East Romans stopped paying the tribute. They knew this meant the Huns would soon resume their attacks, and they began to prepare, taking such measures as increasing the number of soldiers manning the frontier forts. At some point probably in 446, Attila sent letters (dictated to one of his Roman secretaries) to Theodosius, asking for the tribute and the return of fugitives. The emperor answered with an offer to send envoys to discuss the matter, but no more.

An engraving from 1823 illustrates a different version of how Attila obtained the "Sword of Mars." Here, it is presented to him by a seer, who was probably believed to have found it through the guidance of her visions.

*Priscus gave the sword a name that his Roman readers would understand; we don't know what the Huns actually called this legendary weapon.

Attila's people were already itching for war and plunder, and now Attila saw no reason to hold them back. In early 447 he led them across the Danube. The frontier forts, even with the extra men, quickly fell to the Huns, as did the first major military base they came to. Attila continued to follow the Danube eastward till he met with a Roman army at the Utus River. The Romans were overwhelmed, their commander killed, and Attila's way into Thrace was clear. Now the Huns rode with all speed for Constantinople. They had learned that an earthquake (on January 27, 447) had shaken the city and brought down a section of its walls—they would never have a better chance to attack the imperial capital.

For his part, Theodosius knew the Huns were on their way, and everyone in Constantinople realized their situation was desperate. But officials hit on the idea of mobilizing the fan clubs of the city's four chariot-racing teams, enlisting them to clear away the rubble, clean out the moats, and rebuild the wall with its gates and towers. The racing fans had the job done by the end of March. Attila arrived too late to take advantage of the earthquake. Moreover, it appears that illness made at least some of his forces unfit for battle as they neared Constantinople. That is the impression we get from a sermon delivered by a churchman named Isaac of Antioch not long afterward:

A fifteenth-century painting of Constantinople shows how well protected the city was by its walls and the sea, but only hints at its size and splendor.

The Hun in the midst of the field heard about thy [Constantinople's] majesty and envied thee, and thy riches kindled in him the desire to come for the plundering of thy treasures. . . . But the sinners drew the bow and put their arrows on the string . . . and the host was on the point of coming quickly—then sickness blew through it and hurled the host into wilderness. . . . He whose heart was strong for battle waxed feeble through sickness. He who was skillful in shooting with the bow, sickness . . . overthrew him—the riders of the steeds slumbered and slept and the cruel army was silenced.

Leading his warriors away from Constantinople, Attila rode south and defeated the East Roman army headquartered at Callipolis, on the small, strategic peninsula that guarded the opening of the seaward approach to the imperial capital. Now the Balkans lay completely undefended, and the Huns were free to plunder Thrace without resistance. They ranged far and wide, and one contingent even rode down into Greece. They raided as far south as Thermopylae, the historic pass where centuries earlier three hundred Spartans had held off a Persian invasion.

The devastation of the eastern Balkans was almost complete, with all but a handful of cities falling to the Huns. Twenty years later, a monk living not far from Constantinople summarized the war of 447 this way: "The barbarian people of the Huns . . . became so strong that they captured more than 100 cities and almost brought Constantinople into danger. . . . There was so much killing and blood-letting that no one could number the dead. They pillaged the churches and monasteries, and slew the monks and [nuns]. . . . They so devastated Thrace that it will never rise again and be as it was before." Another resident of the Eastern Empire summed up his view of the year's events more briefly: "Attila ground almost the whole of Europe into the dust."

THE HUNS' TACTICS WERE THE TRIED AND TRUE METHODS OF MANY STEPPE NOMADS, a kind of shock warfare that was rare in the Greco-Roman world. When Ammianus Marcellinus wrote about how the Huns fought, he was confident that his readers "would have no hesitation in calling them the most terrible of all warriors":

> They enter the battle in tactical formation, while the medley of their voices makes a savage noise. And as they are lightly equipped for swift motion, and unexpected in action, they purposely divide suddenly in scattered bands and attack, rushing around in disorder here and there, dealing terrific slaughter. . . . At first they fight from a distance with arrows. . . . They then gallop over the intervening spaces and fight hand to hand with swords, regardless of their own lives. Then, while their opponents are guarding against wounds from sword thrusts, they throw strips of cloth plaited into nooses [lassos] over their opponents and so entangle them and pin their limbs so that they lose the ability to ride or walk.

THE HUNS AT WAR

Above: "Shock and awe" were said to characterize Hun warfare, leaving indelible marks on its victims.

Under Attila, the Huns became expert not only at cavalry maneuvers but also at siege warfare. Priscus described how the Huns captured the fortress-city of Naissus, in what is now Serbia:

First they brought up wooden platforms mounted on wheels upon which stood men who shot across at the defenders on the ramparts. . . . In order that the men on the platform could fight in safety, they were sheltered by screens woven from willow covered with rawhide and leather to protect them against missiles and flaming darts which might be shot at them. When a large number of machines had been brought up to the wall, the defenders on the battlements gave in because of the crowds of missiles and evacuated their positions. Then the so-called "rams" were brought up. A ram is a very large machine: a beam is suspended by slack chains from timbers which incline together and it is provided with a sharp metal point. . . . Using short ropes attached to the rear, men swing the beam back from the target of the blow and then release it, so that by its force, part of the wall facing it is smashed away. From the wall the defenders threw down wagon-sized boulders which they had got ready when the machines were first brought up to the circuit [wall]. Some of the machines were crushed with the men working them but the defenders could not hold out against the large number of them. Then the attackers brought up scaling ladders. . . . The barbarians entered through the part of the circuit wall broken by the blows of the rams and also by the scaling ladders set up against the parts which were not crumbling and the city was taken.

Above: The terrifying picture of marauding Huns has come down through the centuries, as this twentieth-century painting shows.

The GREAT KING

By AUTUMN 447, THE EAST ROMANS GAVE UP HOPE OF defending against the Huns in the Balkans and asked for peace. Attila's terms were stern. As usual, he required the return of Hun fugitives and the payment of ransom money for Roman prisoners. He also demanded 6,000 pounds of gold to make up for the tribute that had not been paid, and raised the amount of future tribute to 2,100 pounds a year. And there was one other thing Attila required: a buffer zone or "no man's land" between his kingdom and the Eastern Empire. Specifically, he wanted a strip of land "five days' journey wide" along the south bank of the Danube to be completely evacuated—no forts, no farms, no Romans in the area for any reason. The emperor's negotiators agreed. As Priscus wrote, "because of the overwhelming fear which gripped their commanders they were compelled to accept gladly every injunction, however harsh, in their eagerness for peace." This surrender may be what led the churchman Nestorius to write:

Opposite page: An imposing stained-glass portrait of Attila, made in France in 1883. Attila's reputation through the years has not always been negative. Many modern Hungarians and Turks regard him and his Huns as heroic ancestors.

Because the people of the [Huns] were great and many and formerly were divided into peoples and into kingdoms and were treated as robbers, they used not to do much wrong except only as through rapacity [greed] and through speed; yet later they made them a kingdom and, after they were established in a kingdom, they grew very strong, so that they surpassed in their greatness all the forces of the Romans.

This gold ring was part of the loot taken from the Balkan Peninsula by Hun raiders. It was found in an archaeological expedition launched after a Hungarian peasant woman showed a museum director a piece of Hun jewelry she had discovered on her farm.

AN EYEWITNESS REPORT

By 449 Attila had sent an embassy to Constantinople to complain that the East Romans were not living up to their bargain: there were still Hun fugitives sheltering within the empire, and there were still Balkan peasants farming in the buffer zone. Theodosius responded by sending a diplomat named Maximinus to try to smooth things out with the king of the Huns. Maximinus did not travel alone. Among his companions were an interpreter named Vigilas (or Bigilas) and a junior diplomat—Priscus, the future historian. These East Romans were accompanied on their journey by Attila's ambassadors, Orestes and Edeco. Orestes, originally from Roman Pannonia, was one of Attila's secretaries, while Edeco (or Edecon) was one of Attila's trusted lieutenants and also, apparently, a man of high rank among the Sciri, a Germanic tribe ruled by the Huns.

It took about a month for the party to reach Hun territory, where Edeco rode ahead to inform Attila of the Romans' arrival. Two Hun guides soon met up with them and escorted them to Attila's camp. Writing about his adventures later, Priscus recalled, "When we wished to pitch our tent on a hill the barbarians who met us prevented us, because the tent of Attila was on low ground"—it would have been a tremendous insult for anyone to place their tent higher than the king's. The Romans had to constantly guard themselves against such slipups.

The embassy did not go well. At first Attila wanted to send the Romans away without even seeing them. When they finally did get an audience with Attila, he tore into Vigilas, "calling him a shameless beast, and asking him why he ventured to come when all the deserters had not been given up." Vigilas immediately left for Constantinople, supposedly to find some fugitives whom Attila particularly wanted returned. In reality, Vigilas was going to fetch gold that had been promised to Edeco, whom he had involved in a plot to assassinate Attila. But unknown to Vigilas, once Edeco had returned to the Hun kingdom, he refused to carry out the plan and in fact had told Attila about the whole thing.

Not realizing any of this at the time, Priscus and Maximinus were baffled by Attila's behavior. He put off any other negotiations, and they were forced to follow him from camp to camp for some time. Finally,

We arrived at a large village, where Attila's home was said to be more splendid than his residences in other places. It was made of polished boards, and surrounded with a wooden enclosure, designed, not for protection, but for appearance. . . . When Attila

EX
PRISCI RHETORIS
ET SOPHISTÆ GOTHICA
HISTORIA EXCERPTA, QVÆ LEGA-
tionem Theodofij Iunioris ad Attillam
continent, & plæraque alia.

CAROLO CANTOCLARO CONS.
Regio, & libellorum fupplicum in Regia
Magiftro, interprete.

Eiufdem ad Græca Prifci excerpta Notæ
& Emendationes.

PARISIIS,
Apud ABEL L'ANGELIER, in prima
columna Aulæ Palatij.
M. DC VI.
Cum priuilegio Regis.

Only fragments of Priscus's writings survive. In 1606 they were gathered and published in Paris, with a title page highlighting the fact that the book "contains the legation of Theodosius II to Attila."

entered the village he was met by girls advancing in rows, under thin white canopies of linen, which were held up by the outside women who stood under them, and were so large that seven or more girls walked beneath each. There were many lines of damsels thus canopied, and they sang. . . . When he came near the house of Onegesius [his right-hand man], which lay on his way, the wife of Onegesius issued from the door, with a number of servants, bearing meat and wine, and saluted him and begged him to partake of her hospitality. . . . To gratify the wife of his friend, he ate, just as he sat on his horse, . . . and having tasted the wine, he went on to the palace, which was higher than the other houses and built on an elevated site.

A couple days later Maximinus and Priscus, along with a group of West Roman ambassadors who happened to be there at the same time, received an invitation to a banquet in Attila's palace. They were greeted at the doorway by cupbearers who gave them each a ceremonial drink. As the guests went in to take their places, Priscus looked around with great interest: "All the seats were arranged around the walls of the building. . . . In the very middle of the room Attila sat upon a couch. Behind him was another couch, and behind that steps led up to Attila's bed, which was screened by fine linens and multicoloured ornamental hangings."

The banquet began with more ceremonial drinking. Each guest, in order of importance, was honored with a salute or toast, first by Attila and then by all the other guests. After this ritual was completed, servants brought out the dinner:

While for the other barbarians and for us there were lavishly prepared dishes served on silver platters, for Attila there was

only meat on a wooden plate. . . . Gold and silver goblets were handed to the men at the feast, whereas his cup was of wood. His clothing was plain and differed not at all from that of the rest, except that it was clean. Neither the sword that hung at his side nor the fastenings of his barbarian boots nor his horse's bridle was adorned, like those of the other [Huns], with gold or precious stones.

All things considered, Attila seems to have made a favorable impression on Priscus: "Though a lover of war he was not prone to violence. He was a very wise counsellor, merciful to those who sought it and loyal to those whom he had accepted as friends." Nevertheless, the only real success Maximinus had on this mission was to ransom a Roman lady who had been taken prisoner by the Huns; her children, also captives, were freed without ransom as a gesture of Attila's good will.

As the East Romans headed back to Constantinople, they passed Vigilas along the way. Later Priscus learned that Vigilas was carrying

Two singers entertain Attila (whose youngest son sits beside him) and his guests with songs "celebrating his victories and deeds of valour in war." Priscus noted that some of the audience, men who had grown too old to fight, were moved to tears by these reminders of past glories.

A GREEK AMONG THE HUNS

DURING HIS VISIT TO ATTILA'S HEADQUARTERS, PRISCUS GOT A SURPRISE WHEN ONE OF the Huns addressed him in Greek—"for the subjects of the Huns, swept together from various lands, speak, besides their own barbarous tongues, either Hunnic or Gothic, or—as many have commercial dealings with the western Romans—Latin; but none of them easily speak Greek, except captives . . . and these last are easily known to any stranger by their torn garments and the squalor of their heads." This man, however, was well dressed in Hun-style clothes, with "his hair cut in a circle" like the Huns. He explained that he had been a Greek merchant in a city along the Danube. The city fell to the Huns in 441, and he was taken prisoner by Attila's lieutenant Onegesius. In his master's service, the ex-merchant fought in campaigns against the Romans and then against an independent Hunnic tribe near the Black Sea, and did so well that he earned his freedom.

He then married a barbarian wife and had children, and had the privilege of eating at the table of Onegesius. He considered his new life among the [Huns] better than his old life among the Romans, and the reasons he gave were as follows: "After war the [Huns] live in inactivity, enjoying what they have got, and not at all, or very little, harassed. The Romans, on the other hand, are in the first place very liable to perish in war, as they [civilians] have to rest their hopes of safety on others [the army], and are not allowed . . . to use arms. . . . But the condition of the [Roman] subjects in time of peace is far more grievous than the evils of war, for the exaction of the taxes is very severe, and unprincipled men inflict injuries on others, because the laws are [not applied equally to] all classes."

Above: *For some, the life of the barbarian had the appeal of freedom.*

fifty pounds of gold to pay off Edeco. But Attila took Vigilas prisoner, held him for ransom, kept the gold, and sent a pair of ambassadors to Emperor Theodosius with the empty moneybag and a message: "Theodosius was the son of a nobly born father, and Attila too was of noble descent. . . . But whereas Attila had preserved his noble lineage, Theodosius had fallen from his and was Attila's slave, bound to the payment of tribute. Therefore, in attacking [Attila] covertly like a worthless slave, [Theodosius] was acting unjustly towards his better, whom fortune had made his master."

TURNING WESTWARD

In 450 another team of East Roman ambassadors went to the Huns. After the previous year's diplomatic failures and being called "a worthless slave" by Attila, Theodosius must have been amazed by the success of the new negotiations. Priscus tells us, "Attila swore that he would keep the peace . . . that he would withdraw from the Roman territory bordering the Danube and that he would cease to press the matter of the fugitives . . . providing the Romans did not again receive other fugitives who fled from him." Priscus thought Attila was swayed because the new ambassadors were such high-ranking men and brought him so many splendid gifts that he was overwhelmed by the Eastern Empire's grandness. In reality, though, Attila was hatching some grand plans of his own, which would be easier to carry out knowing that all was secure along the lower Danube.

Attila's kingdom included so much territory and so many peoples now that it could be considered an empire in its own right, and he wanted to grow that empire still more. At first he apparently thought about pushing into Persia, as Basich and Kursich had done back in 395. But no doubt realizing that the Western Empire was an easier target, he headed for Gaul—where the Huns' old friend Aetius had been in charge of the army for most of the past decade. For a long time Aetius had stayed on good terms with Attila, providing him with two of his secretaries. Aetius even gave Attila an honorary office ("master of soldiers"), for which Attila was paid both money and enough grain to feed his warriors in exchange for simply leaving the West Romans alone.

A historian of the time reported that Attila intended to invade Gaul "as guardian of the Romans' friendship," in order to attack the Gothic kingdom ruled from the city of Toulouse—an old enemy of both the Huns and Romans. But relations between Attila and the West Romans had been strained for the past couple years, and they were getting worse. It was said that Honoria, the sister of the Western emperor Valentinian III, had been caught having an affair with a man whom she planned to make emperor so that she could rule at his side. The man was executed, and Honoria was engaged against her will to a respectable, unambitious senator. So she sent a letter to Attila, offering to marry him and give him half the Western Empire. From that point on Attila regarded Honoria as his bride, and threatened Valentinian with vengeance if he interfered with their marriage.

This tension between the Huns and the West Romans increased to breaking point with the death of the king of the Franks, a Germanic confederation along the Rhine River. The Frankish king's two sons quarreled over who should succeed him, and the older son turned to Attila for support, while the younger turned to Aetius. If Attila and Aetius had not definitely been on opposite sides before, they were now.

Attila had all the excuses he needed to go to war, and in the spring of 451 he led a huge army northwest. Unfortunately, few reliable details about the campaign have survived. What is certain is that the Huns and their allies crossed the Rhine into Gaul, where they plundered town and country alike. Eventually they came to the city of Orléans and besieged it.

Legend says that when Attila's Huns tried to attack Paris, they were driven away thanks to the prayers of a nun named Geneviève, who afterward became the city's patron saint.

Meanwhile, Aetius had been marshaling his own troops. He not only had legions from Gaul and Italy under his command, but he had managed to convince the Goths of Toulouse to fight alongside them. The combined Roman-Gothic force caught up with the Huns outside Orléans on June 14. The Huns broke off their seige and headed east toward a place known as the Catalaunian Plains, where there was plenty of the kind of flat, open land where their cavalry could fight most effectively. The Gothic historian Jordanes described the meeting of the two armies there:

> The battlefield was a plain rising by a sharp slope to a ridge, which both armies sought to gain. . . . The Huns with their forces seized the right side, the Romans, the [Goths] and their allies the left. . . . The battleline of the Huns was so arranged that Attila and his bravest followers were in the centre. . . . The innumerable peoples of the diverse tribes, which he had subjected to his sway, formed the wings. . . . The fight grew fierce, confused, monstrous, unrelenting—a fight whose like no ancient time has ever recorded.

The Romans and Goths won a decisive victory that day, although the Goths' king was killed in the battle. But Aetius did not press his advantage, and the Huns were able to retreat back to their own land. There Attila settled down to plan his next campaign.

ANCIENT AUTHORS WHO WROTE ABOUT THE HUNS concerned themselves mainly with warriors and warfare—an activity that Hun women rarely took part in, so far as we know. About the only mention we have of the everyday activities of Hun women comes from Ammianus Marcellinus. Discussing the Huns' nomadic lifestyle in the 370s, he described the wagons "which they make their homes. . . . Their wives live in these wagons, and there weave their miserable garments; and here too they sleep with their husbands, and bring up their children till they reach the age of puberty."

WOMEN OF THE HUNS

From Priscus we learn some things about high-ranking women among the Huns of Attila's kingdom. At one point Priscus visited Attila's chief wife, Hereka, who had her own house in the palace compound: "I . . . found her reclining on a soft couch. The floor was covered with woollen-felt rugs for walking upon. A group of servants stood around her in attendance, and servant girls sat facing her working coloured embroidery on fine linens to be worn as ornaments over the barbarian clothing."

Earlier on their travels, Maximinus and Priscus had been given shelter in a village ruled by Bleda's widow—one of his widows, that is, since Hun leaders had many wives. The ambassadors' tent had blown down in a storm, and they were drenched by the heavy rain. Priscus recalled how the villagers "invited us to their huts and provided warmth for us by lighting large fires of reeds. The lady who governed the village . . . sent us provisions and good-looking girls to console us. . . . We treated the young women to a share in the eatables but declined to take any further advantage of their presence."

We can guess that Bleda's widow was probably not the only "lady who governed." Some women may even have had power over more than a village. A few writings from after the time of Attila mention Hunnic peoples who had female chiefs. In the sixth century, for example, there was Boarex, who took over leadership of a tribe called the Sabiri after her husband died. Unfortunately, this is all we know about her.

Above: This stunning gold funeral mask was buried with a noblewoman from an eastern Hunnic tribe.

Aquileya.

hundert dusent ludes v

koning ezzele vor dan

driv iar. vñ dohe se nicht

nen varen· wan dar he sac

Ezzele·

dar he des landes genar

pauese dar

geschuldeg

vorchte ni

de hadde e

dan he hadde mich trsla

keisere do· dar he eme

ke woren· dar van le

Ezzele.

leo.

5

DEFEATS and DIVISIONS

WHEN SPRING ARRIVED IN 452, ATTILA AND HIS ARMY CROSSED the mountains into northeastern Italy. Their first target was Aquileia, the major city of the region. Aquileia's defenses were strong, however, and the Huns nearly gave up on taking it. But then, as Priscus tells the story, Attila noticed that "the storks, who build their nests in the gables of houses, were bearing their young from the city. . . . He understood this and said to his soldiers: 'You see the birds foresee the future. They are leaving the city sure to perish and are forsaking strongholds doomed to fall. . . . Do not think this a meaningless or uncertain sign.'" Heartened, the Huns carried on their attack, and Aquileia fell to them soon afterward.

Now the fertile Po River valley of northern Italy lay open to the Huns. They tore through this populous region, taking town after town. Then they reached Milan, one of Italy's most important cities, which they successfully besieged. While the Huns were looting Milan, Attila saw there a painting of Roman emperors sitting on golden thrones with

Opposite page: A thirteenth-century manuscript shows Attila (labeled Ezoele, a German form of his name) watching the storks of Aquileia and, later, meeting with Pope Leo.

57

barbarians lying dead at their feet. The sight, according to Priscus, inspired Attila to order a local artist to paint Attila sitting on a throne, with Roman emperors pouring out sacks of gold at *his* feet. Little did he know that there were no more victories ahead for him.

The great sixteenth-century Italian artist Raphael created this image of Pope Leo I's confrontation with Attila to honor Leo X, who was pope from 1513 to 1521.

ATTILA IN ITALY

The Huns sacked Milan but did not destroy it. After a short time they left the city behind, traveling slowly because of their heavy, plunder-filled wagons. Believing that Attila's next target would be Rome itself, Emperor Valentinian sent a three-man embassy to Attila. One of these men was Leo, the bishop of Rome, or pope.

We don't know just what the diplomats said to Attila, but we do know that after this meeting the Huns headed back to the Great Hungarian Plain. Many churchmen later claimed Pope Leo had worked a miracle, or at least had overwhelmed Attila with his holiness and eloquence. One writer, however, indicated that perhaps Attila left because he had gotten what he wanted: on the emperor's behalf, Leo had promised that Honoria would be sent to become Attila's wife, and meanwhile paid him a substantial amount of gold as Honoria's dowry.

There were probably other factors. The chronicler Hydatius wrote, "The Huns who had been plundering Italy and who had also stormed a number of cities, were victims of divine punishment, being visited with heaven-sent disasters: famine and some kind of disease." Famine and disease may not have been divine punishments, but both were likely. The Huns did not have supply lines to assure them of food and other needs, and they were traveling through a region where malaria was a huge problem.

In addition to whatever happened in Italy, it seems that the Huns' lands along the Danube were now under attack. Theodosius II had died in 450, and his powerful sister, Pulcheria, had married a general named Marcian and had him proclaimed emperor of the East. Pulcheria and Marcian decided to stop paying tribute money to Attila, and it looks as though they planned with Aetius to put an end to the threat of the Huns. According to Hydatius, even as the Huns were suffering disease and hunger in northern Italy, "auxiliaries were sent by the emperor Marcian, and under the commandership of Aetius they [the Huns] were slain. Likewise they were subdued in their own [land], partly by plagues from heaven, partly by Marcian's army."

From the sound of it, Attila's campaign of 452 resulted in the deaths of a large number of Huns, both in Italy and at home. Attila may have brought back a lot of gold and plunder, but he did not return to his lands exactly victorious. Between the Battle of the Catalaunian Plains and the latest setbacks, many of his people must have begun to doubt that he would continue to be a successful leader.

THE DEATH OF ATTILA

That autumn Attila sent ambassadors to Marcian threatening that he would "devastate the provinces because that which had been promised him by Theodosius was not paid; the fate of his enemies will be worse than usual." Clearly he planned either to get his tribute from the Eastern Empire or to start raiding it again—he certainly needed gold and victory to keep his warriors' loyalty at this point. It may have been to reinforce bonds of loyalty that he also decided to add a new bride to the wives he already had. She was a Germanic girl named Ildico, probably from a leading family among Attila's subjects or allies.

A medieval German image of Attila's death

The wedding took place in early 453. The historian Jordanes tells what happened after Attila and his new bride were left alone: "He had given himself up to excessive merry-making and he threw himself down on his back heavy with wine and sleep." During the night he suffered a severe nosebleed, "and the blood . . . flowed in its deadly course down his throat, killing him." Rumors would soon arise that Ildico had stabbed him, or that he was poisoned, and that Aetius may have been responsible for plotting his death. Historians still argue about whether or not Attila was murdered. But Attila's own people seemed to accept that his death was from natural causes. Here is Jordanes's description of the funeral:

His body was placed in the midst of a plain and lay in state in a silken tent. . . . The best horsemen of the entire tribe of the Huns rode around in circles . . . in the place to which he had been brought and told of his deeds in a funeral dirge in the following manner: "The chief of the Huns, King Attila, . . . lord of bravest tribes . . . captured cities and terrified both empires of the Roman world. . . . And when he had accomplished all this by the favor of fortune, he fell not by wound of the foe, nor by treachery of friends, but in the midst of his nation at peace, happy in his joy."

THE END OF THE HUN EMPIRE

After the funeral, Jordanes continued, "a contest for the highest place arose among Attila's successors . . . and in their rash eagerness to rule they all alike destroyed his empire." Attila's sons—or at least some of them—seem to have wanted to divide up their father's domain, each of them taking an equal number of the tribes under Hun rule. But it may be that there was also a son (or more than one) who wanted to keep the kingdom whole and rule it all himself. In any case, the sons quarreled. During the resulting conflict one group of Hun subjects, the Gepids, seized the opportunity to rebel. Chaos followed, during which Attila's oldest son was killed in battle.

> An encounter took place between the various nations Attila had held under his sway. Kingdoms with their peoples were divided, and out of one body were made many members. . . . Being deprived of their head, they madly strove against each other. . . . One might see the Goths fighting with pikes, the Gepids raging with the sword, the Rugi breaking off the spears in their own wounds, the Sueves [Suevi] fighting on foot, the Huns with bows, the Alans drawing up a battle-line of heavy-armed and the Herules of light-armed warriors.

Except for the Alans (and of course the Huns), all of the peoples taking part in this struggle were Germanic. It is not clear, however, what side each tribe was fighting on. But it seems that in the end, the subject tribes won their independence from the Huns and no longer had to serve them, pay them tribute, or fight in their army.

It probably took some of these peoples several years to free them-

selves from the Huns. Every time a tribe broke away, Attila's surviving sons lost more power, so they tried to take back control of some peoples. In the late 450s they attacked the Goths settled in Pannonia, whom they regarded as "deserters from their rule, and . . . fugitive slaves." Most of the Hun force was killed, but at least two of Attila's sons got away. A few years later they led another war against the Goths and were again soundly defeated.

Some Goths remained allies or subjects of the Huns a little longer. In the winter of 467–468 Attila's son Dengizich led a band of Huns and Goths across the frozen Danube into Thrace. They seem to have been driven by desperation, and evidently their raids did not bring in enough plunder to support them. Soon the Huns, "hard pressed by starvation and lack of necessities, sent an embassy to the Romans. They said they were ready to surrender, if only they were given land. The Romans answered that they would forward their requests to the emperor. But the barbarians said that they must come to an agreement right away; they were starving and could no longer wait."

This episode was related by Priscus, who went on to describe how a Hun serving in the Roman army stirred up trouble between the Goths and the Huns till battle broke out between them. One band of Huns was slaughtered, and then the others "gathered together and turned against the Romans. . . . The barbarians fought courageously. Those who survived broke through the Roman formations and escaped." Fighting and raiding appear to have continued off and on in Thrace until 469. In that year a Roman general killed Dengizich and sent his head to Constantinople, where, according to an anonymous chronicler, "the whole city turned out to look at it."

Attila's only remaining son (as far as we know) was the youngest, Hernac (or Ernas). Back when Priscus visited Attila's headquarters, he was told "prophets had forewarned Attila that his race would fall, but would be restored by this boy." Hernac did not manage to fulfill the prophecy, but he did lead his followers to safety. With Roman permission, they settled along the Danube in what is now northern Romania. They probably served the Eastern Empire as mercenaries or auxiliaries, their descendants gradually blending in with the peoples of the region. Similarly, other surviving Huns must have settled down in the Balkans or among the Germanic tribes north of the Danube, or they may have joined with steppe raiders who began to appear at the Eastern Empire's edge toward the end of the fifth century. In any case, within less than a hundred years the Huns would no longer exist as a distinct people.

They did leave some interesting legacies, however. For one thing, Hun mercenaries and auxiliaries introduced a new type of soldier into the East Roman army, as a sixth-century historian described:

The bowmen of the present time go into battle wearing corselets [chest armor] and fitted out with greaves [leg armor] which extend up to the knee. . . . They are expert horsemen, and are able without difficulty to direct their bows to either side while riding at full speed, and to shoot an opponent whether in pursuit or in flight. They draw the bowstring along by the forehead about opposite the right ear, thereby charging the arrow with such an impetus as to kill whoever stands in the way, shield and corselet alike having no power to check its force.

Troops like these helped the East Romans take back territories that had been lost to Goths, Vandals, and other barbarians. As a result the newly strengthened Eastern Empire, soon to be known as the Byzantine Empire, would be a dominant force in Europe for centuries and would survive until 1453.

The Western Empire, on the other hand, was doomed, at least partly because of instability caused by the Huns. The last emperor of the West was a twelve-year-old boy named Romulus Augustulus—the son of Attila's secretary Orestes, who had returned to Pannonia and risen high in the

Romulus Augustulus gives up the throne of the Western Empire, leaving Odovacar to become the king of Rome.

Roman military after Attila's death. Similarly, Attila's lieutenant Edeco seems to have achieved a prominent position among Attila's Germanic former subjects. It was Odovacar, son of Edeco, who deposed Romulus Augustulus in 476. He became the first barbarian king of Rome, perhaps in a way fulfilling Attila's dream at last.

EPILOGUE:

The "WHITE HUNS"

WHILE ATTILA'S HUNS WERE STIRRING THINGS UP IN EUROPE, another group of Huns was causing trouble for the Persians. According to the East Roman historian Procopius, these Huns did "not mingle with any of the Huns known to us, for they occupy a land neither adjoining nor even very near to them." He also remarked that although they were "of the stock of the Huns in fact as well as in name," they were "the only ones among the Huns who have white bodies." It is probably because of this description that they became known as the White Huns. They were also called Hephthalites, after the name of one of their early kings.

By the middle of the fifth century the Hephthalites had migrated from eastern Central Asia into Sogdiana, just northeast of the Sasanian Empire. They continued to push farther west, in the process fighting against the Persians repeatedly. The emperor Peroz waged three unsuccessful campaigns against the Hephthalites. After the second he was forced to pay them a large tribute, and in the third (in 484) he was killed. The Hephthalites now controlled territory from Sogdiana west to the Caspian Sea and south into what is now Afghanistan.

When Peroz's son Kavad was overthrown near the beginning of his reign, he made his way to the Hephthalites. He had lived among them as a hostage during his father's reign and had strong ties with them. They provided Kavad with troops who helped him regain his throne. But under his son, Chosroes I, friendship between the Sasanians and the Hephthalites came to an end. This was because a new nomadic group swept into the region in the 550s: the Turks. After they defeated the main Hephthalite army, Chosroes made an alliance with them, and the Hephthalites' domains ended up being divided between the Turks and the Sasanian Empire.

An Indian army surrounds and defeats the Hunas. This illustration is from a history book published in England around 1910.

Meanwhile, a subdivision of the Hephthalites had invaded India in 455. Indian writings referred to them as Hunas. The Indian ruler Skandagupta repelled the first Huna attack and others that followed. His successors, however, were less fortunate. By 510 the Hunas were so strong that they were able to extend their power far into northern and western India.

In 520 the Chinese traveler Sung Yün visited the Hunas' ruler and reported, "[The Hunas] do not live in towns; their seat of government is a moving camp. . . . A large felt tent is erected for their king, measuring forty feet a side; on the inside, the walls are made of woolen rugs. The king's clothes are of ornamented silk, and he sits on a golden bed of which the feet are in the shape of four golden phoenixes. His chief wife also wears an ornamented silk robe which trails three feet along the ground."

Sung Yün also described how hostile the Hunas were toward India's Buddhists. Indeed, many Buddhist monasteries and monuments were destroyed by the Hunas, who harshly persecuted Buddhists in many cities. One Huna king with a particular reputation for cruelty (to animals as well as people) was defeated in battle and driven north by an Indian prince in 533. But the Hunas would continue to threaten India for another century or so, until they were vanquished once and for all by the great Indian king Harsha (died in 647). Any survivors must have blended into the local population, because after the time of Harsha the Hunas disappeared from history.

KEY DATES FOR THE HUNS IN EUROPE

Aetius, both a friend and enemy of the Huns

430 approximate date of Octar's death during campaign against Burgundians

432–433 Rua helps Aetius regain his position as head of West Roman army

436 approximate date of Rua's death; he is succeeded by Bleda and Attila

437 Huns destroy Burgundian kingdom

438 Bleda and Attila negotiate with East Roman diplomats to receive 700 pounds of gold as annual tribute

439 large number of Aetius's Hun allies killed fighting Goths near Toulouse

440–441 breakdown of treaty between Huns and East Romans

441–442 Huns capture or destroy a series of Roman forts and towns south of the Danube

Attila as the quintessential barbarian

444 or 445 Attila has Bleda killed

447 Attila leads huge raid into Thrace, the region around Constantinople, and Greece; East Romans surrender and agree to pay Attila 2,100 pounds of gold a year

449 Priscus visits Attila's court as part of East Roman embassy

451 Attila invades Gaul, besieges Orléans; defeated by Aetius and Goths at Battle of Catalaunian Plains

452 Attila invades Italy, captures Aquileia and sacks Milan, meets with Roman embassy including Pope Leo I; Aetius coordinates Roman attack against Huns both in Italy and on Great Hungarian Plain

453 death of Attila; Huns' Germanic subjects begin to break away

late 450s Attila's sons fight to bring groups of Goths back under Hun rule

467–468 Attila's son Dengizich leads his followers into Thrace, asks for lands in East Roman Empire

469 Dengizich killed in battle with Romans

470s Attila's son Hernac and his followers receive permission to settle in Roman territory

GLOSSARY

Asia Minor A large peninsula surrounded by the Mediterranean, Aegean, and Black seas. Also called Anatolia, it is the part of modern Turkey that lies in Asia.

auxiliaries In the Roman army, forces made up of non-Roman citizens from the provinces or from peoples with whom Rome had treaties.

Balkan Peninsula A peninsula surrounded by the Adriatic, Mediterranean, Aegean, and Black seas. Today it is occupied by the nations of Greece, Macedonia, Albania, Bosnia, Croatia, Slovenia, Yugoslavia, Bulgaria, part of Romania, and the European portion of Turkey.

cavalry Soldiers who fought on horseback.

Gaul The Roman name for the area between the Pyrenees Mountains, the Alps, and the Rhine River—modern France, Belgium, and Luxembourg; most of Switzerland; the westernmost parts of Germany; and the section of the Netherlands that lies south of the Rhine.

Germanic A language family that includes modern German, Dutch, English, Danish, Norwegian, and Swedish as well as the ancient forms of these languages and related languages, including Gothic; can also refer to peoples who spoke Germanic languages and to their culture.

mercenaries Soldiers who hire out their services to anyone willing to pay.

Pannonia The Roman name for the part of Hungary west and south of the Danube River.

regent Someone who takes charge of the government on behalf of a monarch who is too young or too ill to rule.

Thrace The ancient name for the region now occupied by Bulgaria and the European section of Turkey.

FOR MORE INFORMATION

BOOKS

Harvey, Bonnie. *Attila the Hun.* New York: Chelsea House, 2003.

Oliver, Marilyn Tower. *Attila the Hun.* San Diego: Lucent Books, 2006.

Price, Sean Stewart. *Attila the Hun: Leader of the Barbarian Hordes.*
Danbury, CT: Franklin Watts, 2009.

WEB SITES

Attila, King of the Huns.
http://www.boglewood.com/timeline/attila.html

Eye Witness to History. "Dining With Attila the Hun, 448."
http://www.eyewitnesstohistory.com/attila.htm

The History Files. *Barbarian Europe: The Origins of the Huns.*
http://www.historyfiles.co.uk/FeaturesEurope/BarbarianHuns.htm

Miniaev, Sergey. *Xiongnu.*
http://xiongnu.atspace.com/English.htm

Silkroad Foundation. *The White Huns—The Hephthalites.*
http://www.silk-road.com/artl/heph.shtml

SELECTED BIBLIOGRAPHY

Frye, Richard N. *The Heritage of Central Asia: From Antiquity to the
Turkish Expansion.* Princeton: Markus Wiener, 1996.

Grousset, René. *The Empire of the Steppes: A History of Central Asia.*
Translated by Naomi Walford. New Brunswick, NJ: Rutgers University Press, 1970.

Heather, Peter. *The Fall of the Roman Empire: A New History of Rome
and the Barbarians.* New York: Oxford, 2006.

Hildinger, Erik. *Warriors of the Steppe: A Military History of Central
Asia, 500 B.C. to 1700 A.D.* New York: Sarpedon, 1997.

Howarth, Patrick. *Attila, King of the Huns: Man and Myth.* New York: Barnes and Noble, 1995.

Jones, Terry, and Alan Ereira. *Terry Jones' Barbarians.* London: BBC Books, 2006.

Kennedy, Hugh. *Mongols, Huns and Vikings: Nomads at War.* London: Cassell, 2002.

Legg, Stuart. *The Barbarians of Asia: The Peoples of the Steppes from 1600 B.C.* 1970. reprint, New York: Dorset Press, 1990.

Maenchen-Helfen, Otto J. *The World of the Huns: Studies in Their History and Culture.* Berkeley: University of California Press, 1973.

Man, John. *Attila: The Barbarian King Who Challenged Rome.* New York: St. Martin's Press, 2006.

McCullough, David Willis, ed. *Chronicles of the Barbarians: Firsthand Accounts of Pillage and Conquest, From the Ancient World to the Fall of Constantinople.* New York: Times Books, 1998.

Thompson, E. A. *The Huns.* Malden, MA: Blackwell Publishing, 1999.

Yarshater, Ehsan, ed. *Encyclopaedia Iranica.*
http://www.iranica.com/newsite

SOURCES FOR QUOTATIONS

Chapter 1

p. 9 "a race of men": McCullough, *Chronicles of the Barbarians*, p. xiii.

p. 9 "absolutely unacquainted": Maenchen-Helfen, *The World of the Huns*, p. 376.

p. 13 "My family married me": from *World Poetry: An Anthology of Verse from Antiquity to Our Time*, edited by Katharine Washburn and John S. Major (New York: Norton, 1998), pp. 196–197.

p. 14 "Whenever a Xiongnu": Yarshater, *Encyclopaedia Iranica*, "Xiongnu."

p. 14 "They have no desire": Legg, *The Barbarians of Asia*, p. 93.

p. 16 "Heaven was pitiless": from *The Penguin Book of Women Poets*,
edited by Carol Cosman et al. (New York: Penguin Books, 1979), p. 49.

Chapter 2

p. 21 "those barbarians who": Thompson, *The Huns*, p. 26.

p. 21 "a terrible rumour": McCullough, *Chronicles of the Barbarians*,
p. 126.

p. 22 "the seed-bed and origin": Heather, *The Fall of the Roman
Empire*, p. 146.

p. 22 "having traversed": McCullough, *Chronicles of the Barbarians*,
p. 125.

p. 23 "the barbarians, like beasts": ibid., p. 135.

p. 24 "spreading ravage": ibid., p. 134.

p. 24 "roving fierceness" and "more violent": Thompson, *The Huns*,
p. 30.

p. 25 "accepted the barbarian": Maenchen-Helfen, *The World of the
Huns*, p. 45.

p. 26 "O memorable thing": ibid., p. 45.

p. 27 "the bridge was cut off": ibid., p. 58.

p. 27 "Lo, suddenly messengers": Thompson, *The Huns*, pp. 31–32.

p. 28 "Basich and Kursich": Maenchen-Helfen, *The World of the
Huns*, p. 54.

p. 28 "They descended": ibid., p. 58.

p. 29 "savage tribes": ibid., p. 64.

p. 30 "were totally incapable": Heather, *The Fall of the Roman
Empire*, p. 155.

p. 30 "Scarcely has the infant": Kennedy, *Mongols, Huns and Vikings*,
p. 29.

p. 31 "The Hunnish horses": Howarth, *Attila, King of the Huns*, pp.
19–20.

Chapter 3

p. 34 "John sent Aetius": Maenchen-Helfen, *The World of the Huns*, p.77.

p. 34 "burst asunder" and "the Burgundians attacked": ibid., p. 83.

p. 36 "think it proper": Heather, *The Fall of the Roman Empire*, pp. 300–301.

p. 37 "the bishop of Margus": ibid., p. 301.

p. 39 "A certain herdsman": Man, *Attila*, p. 139.

p. 41 "The Hun in the midst": Maenchen-Helfen, *The World of the Huns*, p. 122.

p. 41 "The barbarian people": Man, *Attila*, p. 150.

p. 41 "Attila ground": Thompson, *The Huns*, p. 103.

p. 42 "would have no hesitation": Kennedy, *Mongols, Huns and Vikings*, p. 28.

p. 42 "They enter the battle": ibid., pp. 27–28.

p. 43 "First they brought up": ibid., pp. 31–34.

Chapter 4

p. 45 "five days' journey": Maenchen-Helfen, *The World of the Huns*, p. 124.

p. 45 "because of the overwhelming": Heather, *The Fall of the Roman Empire*, p. 312.

p. 46 "Because the people": Thompson, *The Huns*, p. 68.

p. 46 "When we wished": McCullough, *Chronicles of the Barbarians*, p. 153.

p. 47 "calling him a shameless": ibid., p. 154.

p. 47 "We arrived at a large village": ibid., p. 157.

p. 48 "All the seats": Heather, *The Fall of the Roman Empire*, p. 318.

p. 48 "While for the other": ibid., p. 320.

p. 49 "Though a lover of war": ibid., p. 319.

p. 50 "for the subjects" and "his hair cut": McCullough, *Chronicles of the Barbarians*, p. 158.

p. 50 "He then married": ibid., pp. 158–159.

p. 51 "Theodosius was the son": Heather, *The Fall of the Roman Empire*, pp. 323–324.

p. 51 "Attila swore": ibid., p. 334.

p. 52 "as guardian": Thompson, *The Huns*, p. 144.

p. 54 "The battlefield was": Heather, *The Fall of the Roman Empire*, p. 339.

p. 55 "which they make": McCullough, *Chronicles of the Barbarians*, p. 123.

p. 55 "I . . . found her": Heather, *The Fall of the Roman Empire*, p. 318.

p. 55 "invited us to their huts": McCullough, *Chronicles of the Barbarians*, p. 155.

Chapter 5

p. 57 "the storks": Maenchen-Helfen, *The World of the Huns*, p. 133.

p. 58 "The Huns who had been": Heather, *The Fall of the Roman Empire*, pp. 340–341.

p. 59 "auxiliaries were sent": Maenchen-Helfen, *The World of the Huns*, pp. 137–138.

p. 59 "devastate the provinces": ibid., p. 143.

p. 60 "He had given" and "and the blood": Man, *Attila*, p. 262.

p. 60 "His body was placed": McCullough, *Chronicles of the Barbarians*, p. 176.

p. 61 "a contest for the highest": ibid., p. 177.

p. 61 "An encounter took place": Heather, *The Fall of the Roman Empire*, p. 354.

p. 62 "deserters from their rule": Thompson, *The Huns*, p. 169.

p. 62 "hard pressed by starvation": Maenchen-Helfen, *The World of the Huns*, p. 167.

p. 63 "gathered together and turned": ibid., pp. 167–168.

p. 63 "the whole city": ibid., p. 168.

p. 63 "prophets had forewarned": McCullough, *Chronicles of the Barbarians*, p. 164.

p. 63 "The bowmen of the present": Hildinger, *Warriors of the Steppe*, p. 73.

Epilogue

p. 65 "not mingle," "of the stock," and "the only ones": Howarth, *Attila, King of the Huns*, p. 26.

p. 66 "[The Hunas] do not live": Grousset, *The Empire of the Steppes*, p. 70.

INDEX

Page numbers for illustrations are in boldface

ABOUT THE AUTHOR

Kathryn Hinds grew up near Rochester, New York. She studied music and writing at Barnard College, and went on to do graduate work in  comparative literature and medieval studies at the City University of New York. She has written more than forty books for young people, including *Everyday Life in Medieval Europe* and the books in the series LIFE IN THE MEDIEVAL MUSLIM WORLD, LIFE IN ELIZABETHAN ENGLAND, LIFE IN ANCIENT EGYPT, LIFE IN THE ROMAN EMPIRE, and LIFE IN THE RENAISSANCE. Kathryn lives in the north Georgia mountains with her husband, their son, and an assortment of cats and dogs. When she is not reading or writing, she enjoys dancing, gardening, knitting, playing music, and taking walks in the woods. Visit Kathryn online at www.kathrynhinds.com